EVERYDAY PATTERNS

Compiled by Jean Warren
Illustrated by Gary Mohrmann

Warren Publishing House, Inc.
Everett, Washington

Editorial Staff: Gayle Bittinger, Susan M. Sexton, Jean Warren

Production Manager: Eileen Carbary

Design: Kathy Jones

Cover–Computer Graphics: Kathy Jones and Eric Stovall

ISBN: 0-911019-35-9

Printed in the United States of America
Published by: Warren Publishing House, Inc.
        P.O. Box 2250
        Everett, Washington 98203

CONTENTS

Using Everyday Patterns

Mix and match the patterns in this book to create a variety of teaching props, learning games, bulletin boards and more. Following are some suggestions of ways to use the patterns. Adapt these ideas or make up your own — the only limit is your imagination.

Language

Flannelboard Story Characters — Use the patterns as guides to cut everyday shapes out of felt or construction paper backed with felt strips.

Stick Puppets — Color and cut out photocopies of the smallest everyday shapes and glue them to Popsicle sticks or tongue depressors.

Stand-up Story Characters — Use the patterns as guides to cut everyday shapes out of posterboard. Make stands for the shapes out of posterboard or playdough.

Magnetic Story Character — Use the patterns as guides to cut everyday shapes out of construction paper or posterboard and attach magnets to the backs of them.

Picture Books — Photocopy several everyday shapes of the same size, arrange them in the desired order and staple them together to make books. Add construction paper covers, if desired.

Draw-A-Story — Cut out several photocopied shapes, cover them with clear self-stick paper and put them in a bag or a box. Let the children take turns pulling out a shape for you to incorporate into a story.

Music and Movement

Finger Puppets — Color and cut out photocopies of the smallest everyday shapes and attach them to construction paper or pipe cleaner "rings." Use the finger puppets while reciting poems or singing everyday songs.

Everyday Songs — Use the patterns as guides to cut everyday shapes out of construction paper or felt. Use the shapes as props while singing songs or telling stories.

Art

Stencils — Use the patterns as guides to cut everyday shapes out of large pieces of posterboard or tag board to make stencils.

Necklaces — Use the patterns as guides to cut everyday shapes out of construction paper. Let the children each decorate one or more shapes. Have the children string their shapes on pieces of yarn.

Stamps — Use the patterns as guides to cut everyday shapes out of sponges. Glue the sponge shapes to blocks of wood to make stamps.

Classroom Aids

Room Decorations — Use the patterns as guides to cut out everyday shapes for decorating bulletin boards or creating a frieze.

Calendar Markers — Use one of the smaller patterns as a guide to cut everyday shapes, one for each day of the month, out of construction paper. Number the shapes and arrange them in a calendar format on a bulletin board.

Name Tags — Use the patterns as guides to cut everyday shapes out of construction paper. Write a child's name on each shape and string it on a piece of yarn.

Learning Games

Matching — Use the patterns as guides to cut various sizes and kinds of everyday shapes out of various colors of construction paper or felt. Let the children match the shapes by size, kind or color.

Counting — Use the patterns as guides to cut various sizes and kinds of everyday shapes out of various colors of construction paper or felt. Ask the children to count the large shapes, the red shapes or all of the car shapes.

Sizing — Use the patterns as guides to cut four sizes of one object's shape out of construction paper or felt. Have the children arrange the shapes by size.

Sorting — Use the patterns as guides to cut various sizes and kinds of everyday shapes out of various colors of construction paper or felt. Let the children sort the shapes by size, kind, color or type.

Card Games — Photocopy and cut out the game cards. Cover them with clear self-stick paper. Help the children use the cards to play such games as Go Fish, Concentration, Lotto and Bingo.

Astronaut's Helmet 7

Astronaut's Helmet 9

Baseball Cap 11

Baseball Cap 13

Chef's Hat 15

Chef's Hat 17

Firefighter's Helment 19

Firefighter's Helment 21

Police Officer's Hat   27

Police Officer's Hat   29

Rain Hat 33

Top Hat 37

Western Hat 41

Bed 43

Bed 45

Bowl 53

Chair 57

Comb 59

Comb 61

Computer 63

Computer 65

Cup 71

Cup 73

Hairbrush 77

Key 81

Lamp 83

Lamp 85

Plate 87

Plate 89

Table 95

Table 97

Telephone 101

Baby 111

Boy 115

Boy 117

Girl 119

Girl 121

Man 125

Woman   127

Woman 129

Bat 135

Bat 137

Doll 139

Doll 141

Drum 143

Drum 145

Horn   151

Kite 157

Teddy Bear 163

Teddy Bear 165

Top 167

Wagon 173

Bicycle 175

Camper 185

Car 189

Fire Engine 193

Hot Air Balloon   195

Hot Air Balloon 197

Jet 201

Police Car 209

Rocket 211

Rocket 213

Sailboat 215

Sailboat 217

Ship 219

Tractor 223

Train Caboose 227

Train Caboose 229

Tricycle 235

INDEX

Activities, songs and new ideas to use right now are waiting for you in every issue of the

TOTLINE® NEWSLETTER.

Each issue puts the fun into teaching with 24 pages of challenging and creative activities for young children, including open-ended art activities, learning games, music language and science activities.

Sample Issue $1.00

You'll find the *Totline® Newsletter* an indispensable source of fresh new ideas. Page for page, there are more usable activities in this newsletter than in any other early childhood education newsletter.

"Out of all the materials on the market today, I find your resources are what I use."

"...The ideas are very refreshing."

"It's the finest magazine for the preschool teachers that I've found in my 12 years of teaching."

"For my money spent, I get more ideas from your newsletter than any other publication I receive."

"I love the Totline® Newsletter. I just keep finding new resources and ideas to keep me fresh."

Additional information or sample orders write to:
Warren Publishing House, Inc., P.O. Box 2250, Dept. B, Everett, WA 98203

Totline Books

Super Snacks - 120 seasonal sugarless snack recipes kids love.

Teaching Tips - 300 helpful hints for working with young children.

Teaching Toys - over 100 toy and game ideas for teaching learning concepts.

Piggyback Songs - 110 original songs, sung to the tunes of childhood favorites.

More Piggyback Songs - 195 more original songs.

Piggyback Songs for Infants and Toddlers - 160 original songs, for infants and toddlers.

Piggyback Songs in Praise of God - 185 original religious songs, sung to familiar tunes.

Piggyback Songs in Praise of Jesus - 240 more original religious songs.

Holiday Piggyback Songs - over 240 original holiday songs.

Animal Piggyback Songs - over 200 original songs about animals.

1·2·3 Art - over 200 open-ended art activities.

1·2·3 Games - 70 no-lose games to ages 2 to 8.

1·2·3 Colors - over 500 Color Day activities for young children.

1·2·3 Puppets - over 50 puppets to make for working with young children.

1·2·3 Murals - over 50 murals to make with children's open-ended art.

1·2·3 Books - over 20 beginning concept books to make for working with young children.

Teeny-Tiny Folktales - 15 folktales from around the world plus flannelboard patterns.

Short-Short Stories - 18 original stories plus seasonal activities.

Mini-Mini Musicals - 10 simple musicals, sung to familiar tunes.

Small World Celebrations - 16 holidays from around the world to celebrate with young children.

Special Day Celebrations - 55 mini celebrations for holidays and special events.

Yankee Doodle Birthday Celebrations - activity ideas for celebrating birthdays of 30 famous Americans.

"Cut & Tell" Scissor Stories for Fall - 8 original stories plus patterns.

"Cut & Tell" Scissor Stories for Winter - 8 original stories plus patterns.

"Cut & Tell" Scissor Stories for Spring - 8 original stories plus patterns.

Seasonal Fun - 50 two-sided reproducible parent flyers.

Theme-A-Saurus - the great big book of mini teaching themes.

Theme-A-Saurus II - the great big book of more mini teaching themes.

Alphabet and Number Rhymes - reproducible take-home books.

Color, Shape & Season Rhymes - reproducible take-home books.

Object Rhymes - reproducible take-home books about seasonal objects such as hearts, pumpkins and turkeys.

Animal Rhymes - reproducible pre-reading books using repetition and rhyme about animals.

Our World - more than 120 easy environmental activities.

"Mix & Match" Animal Patterns - multi-sized patterns for 58 different animals.

"Mix & Match" Everyday Patterns - multi-sized patterns for 58 different everyday objects.

"Mix & Match" Nature Patterns - multi-sized patterns for 58 different nature objects.

Available at school supply stores and parent/teacher stores or write for our *FREE* catalog.

Warren Publishing House, Inc. • P.O. Box 2250, Dept. B • Everett, WA 98203